5/14

FOSSIL RIDGE PUBLIC LIBRARY DISTRICT

W9-BVL-601

mapping NORTH AMERICA

FOSSIL RIDGE PUBLIC LIBRARY DISTRICT
BRAIDWOOD, IL 60408

Gareth Stevens
Publishing

By Emily Jankowski

Please visit our website, www.garethstevens.com. For a free color catalog of all our high-quality books, call toll free 1-800-542-2595 or fax 1-877-542-2596.

Library of Congress Cataloging-in-Publication Data

Jankowski, Emily.
Mapping North America / by Emily Jankowski.
 p. cm. — (Mapping the world)
Includes index.
ISBN 978-1-4339-9115-8 (pbk.)
ISBN 978-1-4339-9116-5 (6-pack)
ISBN 978-1-4339-9114-1 (library binding)
1. North America—Geography—Juvenile literature. 2. North America—Juvenile literature. 3. Cartography—North America—Juvenile literature. I. Title.
GA401.J36 2014
970—dc23

First Edition

Published in 2014 by
Gareth Stevens Publishing
111 East 14th Street, Suite 349
New York, NY 10003

Copyright © 2014 Gareth Stevens Publishing

Designer: Katelyn E. Reynolds
Editor: Kristen Rajczak

Photo credits: Cover, p. 1 (photo) Mariia Sats/Shutterstock.com; cover, pp. 1, 5 (map) Uwe Dedering/Wikipedia.com; cover, pp. 1-24 (banner) kanate/Shutterstock.com; cover, pp. 1-24 (series elements and cork background) iStockphoto/Thinkstock.com; pp. 5 (compass rose), 11 (inset) iStockphoto/Thinkstock.com; pp. 7, 17 (inset) Globe Turner/Shutterstock.com; p. 9 (inset) Hulton Archive/Getty Images; p. 9 (main) NuclearVacuum/Wikipedia.com; p. 11 (main) E Pluribus Anthony at the English Wikipedia project; p. 13 (inset) Gail Johnson/Shutterstock.com; pp. 13 (main), 15 (inset) AridOcean/Shutterstock.com; p. 15 (main) Mauricio Avramow/Shutterstock.com; p. 17 (main) Michele Falzone/AWL Images/Getty Images; p. 19 (inset) Tom Pfeiffer/VolcanoDiscovery/Flickr/Getty Images; p. 19 (main) Cacahuate, translations by Joelf and Globe-trotter/Wikipedia.com; p. 21 (inset) Donald Erickson/E+/Getty Images; p. 21 (main) dalmingo/Shutterstock.com.

All rights reserved. No part of this book may be reproduced in any form without permission in writing from the publisher, except by a reviewer.

Printed in the United States of America

CPSIA compliance information: Batch #CS13GS: For further information contact Gareth Stevens, New York, New York at 1-800-542-2595.

CONTENTS

Words in the glossary appear in **bold** type the first time they are used in the text.

WHAT IS NORTH AMERICA?

North America is the world's third-largest **continent**. It's bordered to the north by the Arctic Ocean and to the east by the Atlantic Ocean. The Pacific Ocean borders it to the west and south. To the southeast are South America and the Caribbean Sea.

The **equator** separates the Northern and Southern **Hemispheres**. North America is above the equator, so it's in the Northern Hemisphere. This continent is home to islands, mountains, rivers, lakes, deserts, rainforests, and much more!

Where in the World?

North America is home to almost 550 million people!

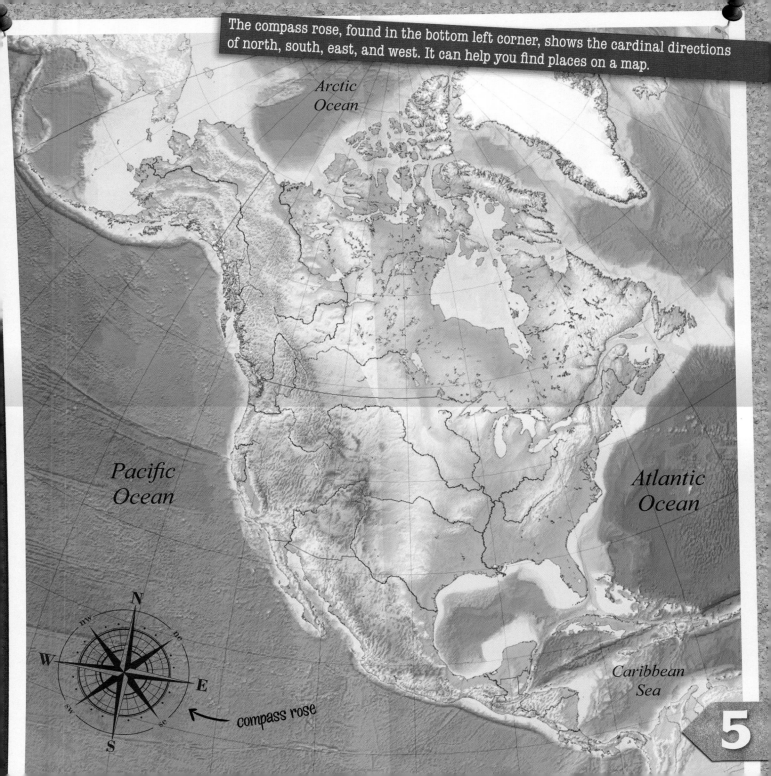

The compass rose, found in the bottom left corner, shows the cardinal directions of north, south, east, and west. It can help you find places on a map.

Arctic
Ocean

Pacific
Ocean

Atlantic
Ocean

Caribbean
Sea

N

nw   ne

W   E

sw   se

S

compass rose

COUNTRIES IN NORTH AMERICA

The countries in North America include the United States of America, Canada, and Mexico. The Caribbean islands, countries of Central America, and Greenland are also part of North America. Many of the people in these countries speak English, but they also speak French, Spanish, and Dutch.

The map on the next page is called a political map. It shows each country's borders. Sometimes, landforms form natural borders between nations. The Rio Grande forms part of the border between the United States and Mexico.

Where in the World?

In North America, Canada is the largest country by area, but the United States is home to the most people.

170°
180°
170°
Bering Strait
Bering Sea
160°
150°
140°
130°

Arctic Circle
Chukchi Sea
0°
160°
140°
120°
100°
80°
Arctic Ocean
60°
40°
20°
10°

ICELAND
GREENLAND
(Den.)
Denmark Strait
Arctic Circle
20°

Beaufort Sea
Baffin Bay
Davis Strait
30°
50°

Gulf of Alaska
Great Bear L.
Great Slave L.
Athabasca
Hudson Strait
Labrador Sea

CANADA
Hudson Bay
40°

L. Winnipeg
James Bay

L. Superior
Huron
Michigan
Ontario
Erie
50°

UNITED STATES
Bermuda
(U.K.)

30°
ATLANTIC OCEAN

Tropic of Cancer

PACIFIC OCEAN
20°
MEXICO
Gulf of Mexico
Straits of Florida
Bay of Campeche

BAHAMAS
ST. KITTS & NEVIS
BARBADOS
Virgin Is. (U.S., U.K.)
Guadeloupe (Fr.)
Puerto Rico (U.S.)
ANTIGUA & BARBUDA
Turks & Caicos Is. (U.K.)
CUBA
DOMINICA
HAITI
Martinique (Fr.)
Cayman Is. (U.K.)
ST. LUCIA
DOMINICAN REPUBLIC
ST. VINCENT & THE GRENADINES
JAMAICA
Curaçao (Neth.)
GRENADA
Aruba (Neth.)
TRINIDAD & TOBAGO
Bonaire (Neth.)
60°

BELIZE
Caribbean Sea
130°
GUATEMALA
HONDURAS
NICARAGUA
EL SALVADOR
COSTA RICA
PANAMA

Gulf of California
Tropic of Cancer
140°

7

AMERIGO VESPUCCI

North America is named after an Italian **explorer** named Amerigo Vespucci. He tried to find a shorter way to sail to Asia in the late 1400s and early 1500s. Vespucci was one of the first people to believe that the land he visited was part of a new continent—not part of Asia, like many others believed.

Vespucci claimed to have made four trips back and forth from Europe to North America. However, some historians say it may have been only two.

Where in the World?

Amerigo Vespucci knew another early explorer named Christopher Columbus. He helped Columbus get ready for his second and third **voyages**.

Although the land Amerigo Vespucci visited was in South America, both North America and South America are named after him.

North America

Europe

Africa

South America

Vespucci's Voyages
1499–1500
1501–1502
1503–1504

Amerigo Vespucci

CANADA

Canada is the largest country in North America. It's made up of 13 different parts. Ten are called provinces, and three are territories. A prime minister elected by the people of Canada is head of the country's government.

Toronto, Montreal, Calgary, and Edmonton are some of the largest cities in Canada. Their citizens speak English, but many also speak French. Much of Canada is wilderness and forest, making it a great place to hunt and fish.

Where in the World?

Niagara Falls is one of Canada's best-known attractions. It's the largest waterfall in the world, measured in the amount of water that flows over it.

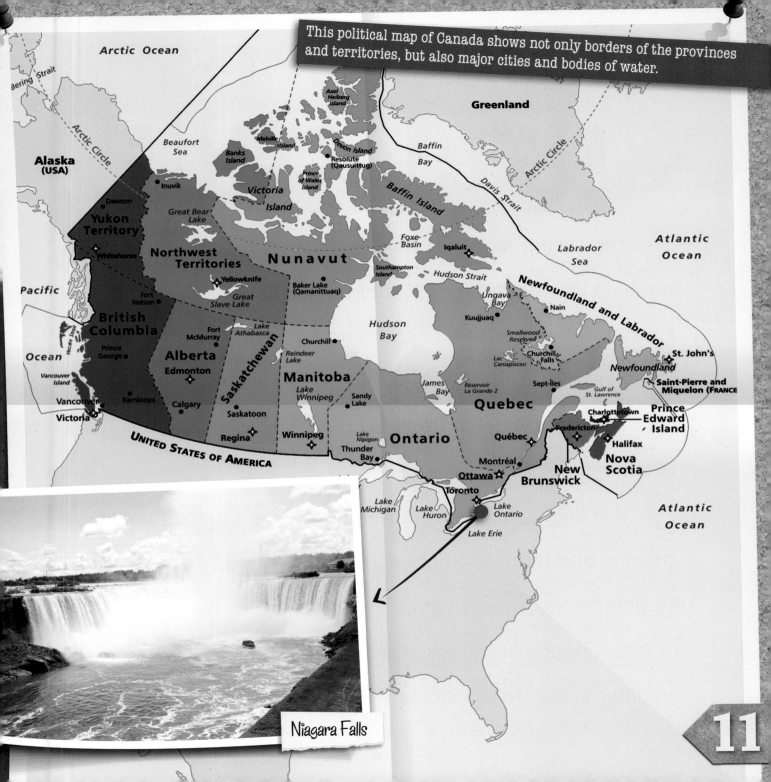

This political map of Canada shows not only borders of the provinces and territories, but also major cities and bodies of water.

Arctic Ocean

Bering Strait

Arctic Circle

Alaska (USA)

Beaufort Sea

Greenland

Banks Island

Melville Island

Devon Island

Axel Heiberg Island

Resolute (Qausuittug)

Baffin Bay

Arctic Circle

Dawson

Inuvik

Yukon Territory

Victoria Island

Prince of Wales Island

Baffin Island

Davis Strait

Whitehorse

Northwest Territories

Great Bear Lake

Nunavut

Foxe Basin

Iqaluit

Labrador Sea

Atlantic Ocean

Pacific

Yellowknife

Great Slave Lake

Baker Lake (Qamanittuaq)

Southampton Island

Hudson Strait

Newfoundland and Labrador

Ocean

Fort Nelson

British Columbia

Fort McMurray

Lake Athabasca

Hudson Bay

Ungava Bay

Kuujjuaq

Nain

Smallwood Reservoir

Prince George

Alberta

Saskatchewan

Reindeer Lake

Churchill

Churchill Falls

Lac Caniapiscau

Newfoundland

St. John's

Vancouver Island

Edmonton

Manitoba

Lake Winnipeg

Sandy Lake

James Bay

Réservoir La Grande 2

Sept-Îles

Gulf of St. Lawrence

Saint-Pierre and Miquelon (FRANCE)

Vancouver

Kamloops

Calgary

Saskatoon

Quebec

Charlottetown

Prince Edward Island

Victoria

Regina

Winnipeg

Lake Nipigon

Ontario

Québec

Fredericton

Halifax

Nova Scotia

UNITED STATES OF AMERICA

Thunder Bay

Montréal

Ottawa

New Brunswick

Toronto

Lake Michigan

Lake Huron

Lake Ontario

Atlantic Ocean

Lake Erie

Niagara Falls

11

THE UNITED STATES OF AMERICA

The United States of America is in the middle of North America. It's made up of 50 states, including Alaska and Hawaii. The states are all different from each other, with weather ranging from hot, **humid** summers in Florida to cold winters in Alaska. Texas is commonly sunny, while Washington State is rainy.

The Rocky Mountains are in the western part of the country, and the Appalachian Mountains are in the east. Both of these mountain ranges impact weather in the United States.

Where in the World?

At the beginning of 2013, about 315 million people were living in the United States. The largest city is New York, New York.

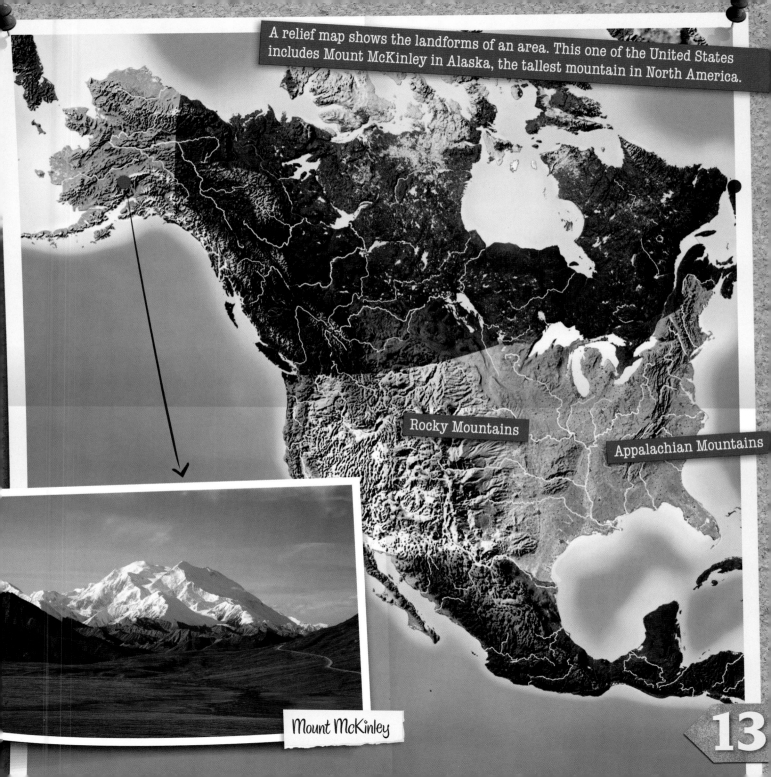

A relief map shows the landforms of an area. This one of the United States includes Mount McKinley in Alaska, the tallest mountain in North America.

Rocky Mountains

Appalachian Mountains

Mount McKinley

13

MEXICO

Mexico is located between the United States and Central America. It's about one-fifth of the size of the United States. Mexico's capital, Mexico City, is also one of the most populous cities in the world.

The high Mexican **Plateau** makes up a large part of the country's center. To the east and west are large mountain ranges. Because of the dry, mountainous land, many parts of Mexico don't grow crops well. However, wheat, corn, and beans are often grown where the soil is good.

Where in the World?

Mexico is located in the Ring of Fire. This area around the Pacific Ocean is one of Earth's most active **volcano** zones.

Mexico City lies in a basin called the Valley of Mexico. People have lived in this area for thousands of years!

Mexico City

THE CARIBBEAN

There are more than 7,000 small islands in the Caribbean! Sometimes they're called the West Indies because Christopher Columbus thought he'd reached the Indies of Asia. All these islands are located in the Atlantic Ocean and the Caribbean Sea. Some islands are their own country, such as Jamaica, Cuba, and Barbados.

The Caribbean islands are very close to the equator. They're known for their beautiful beaches, palm trees, and **tropical** weather. Many people like to vacation here.

Where in the World?

Some islands, such as the British and US Virgin Islands, are run by other nations.

Tropic of Cancer

BAHAMAS

Straits of Florida

ST. KITTS & NEVIS
Virgin Is. (U.S., U.K.)
Puerto Rico
(U.S.)
Turks &
Caicos Is. (U.K.)

20°

BARBADOS
Guadeloupe
ANTIGUA & (Fr.)
BARBUDA

CUBA

HAITI

Cayman Is.
(U.K.)

JAMAICA

DOMINICAN
REPUBLIC
Curaçao
(Neth.)
Aruba
(Neth.)

DOMINICA
Martinique (Fr.)
ST. LUCIA
ST. VINCENT &
THE GRENADINES
GRENADA
TRINIDAD
& TOBAGO

Bonaire
(Neth.)

60°

0°

Caribbean Sea

CENTRAL AMERICA

Central America is made up of seven countries: Belize, Guatemala, Honduras, Nicaragua, El Salvador, Costa Rica, and Panama. Considered part of North America, it connects Mexico and South America. Since Central America is close to the equator, it's very warm for most of the year.

Central America has rainforests, beaches, and many mountains. The Andes Mountains start in Central America and continue into South America. The Sierra Madre also runs through this part of North America.

Where in the World?

Nicaragua is the largest country in Central America.

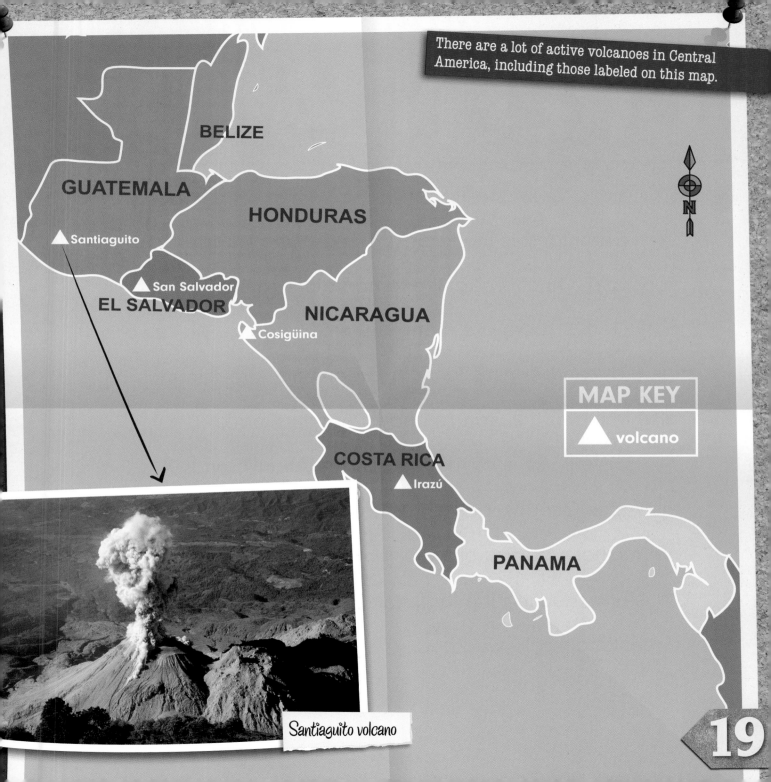

There are a lot of active volcanoes in Central America, including those labeled on this map.

BELIZE

GUATEMALA

HONDURAS

▲ Santiaguito

▲ San Salvador

EL SALVADOR

NICARAGUA

▲ Cosigüina

N

MAP KEY

▲ volcano

COSTA RICA

▲ Irazú

PANAMA

Santiaguito volcano

GREENLAND

Greenland is the largest island in the world! It's also very cold. On average, the temperature rarely goes above 50°F (10°C). There are many icebergs, or large pieces of ice that can be miles long, in Greenland. Greenland is also home to the world's largest national park.

Greenland is surrounded by the Atlantic and the Arctic Oceans, both of which are very cold so far north. These bodies of water are constantly cooling the land, causing Greenland's cold weather.

Where in the World?

Though Greenland is part of Denmark, it has its own government, too.

Fun Facts About North America

The Missouri River in the United States is the longest river in North America.

Lake Superior is the largest freshwater lake in the world. It's located on the border between the United States and Canada.

The highest temperature in North America was recorded in Death Valley, California, in 1913. It reached 134°F (57°C).

The lowest temperature in North America was recorded in Yukon, Canada, in 1947. It dipped to −81°F (−63°C).

There's no spot in Central America more than 125 miles (200 km) from the ocean.

21

GLOSSARY

continent: one of Earth's seven great landmasses. They are Asia, Africa, Europe, Australia, Antarctica, North America, and South America.

equator: an imaginary line around Earth that is the same distance from the North and the South Poles

explorer: someone who travels in order to find out new things

hemisphere: one half of Earth

humid: wet

plateau: an area of level ground that is higher than the ground around it

tropical: having to do with the warm parts of Earth near the equator

volcano: an opening in a planet's surface through which hot, liquid rock sometimes flows

voyage: trip, usually taken on a boat

FOR MORE INFORMATION

Books

Aloian, Molly, and Bobbie Kalman. *Explore North America*. New York, NY: Crabtree Publishing, 2007.

Mara, Wil. *The Seven Continents*. New York, NY: Children's Press, 2005.

Olien, Rebecca. *Map Keys*. New York, NY: Children's Press, 2012.

Websites

How Stuff Works: Maps of North America
maps.howstuffworks.com/maps-of-north-america.htm
Use interactive maps of the different parts of North America to learn more!

World Atlas: North America
www.worldatlas.com/webimage/countrys/na.htm
Use this website to learn more about North America, including fun facts, famous natives, flags, and maps.

Publisher's note to educators and parents: Our editors have carefully reviewed these websites to ensure that they are suitable for students. Many websites change frequently, however, and we cannot guarantee that a site's future contents will continue to meet our high standards of quality and educational value. Be advised that students should be closely supervised whenever they access the Internet.

INDEX

24

FOSSIL RIDGE PUBLIC LIBRARY DISTRICT
BRAIDWOOD, IL 60408

3 2186 00209 9256